How To Ski & Fix Your Knees

Charleston, SC
www.PalmettoPublishing.com

How To Ski & Fix Your Knees
Copyright © 2023 by Dr. Moir Bowman,
D.C., F.I.A.M.A., DIPL. AC (IAMA)

All rights reserved

No portion of this book may be reproduced, stored in a retrieval system, or transmitted in any form by any means—electronic, mechanical, photocopy, recording, or other—except for brief quotations in printed reviews, without prior permission of the author.

Paperback ISBN: 979-8-8229-1923-5
eBook ISBN: 979-8-8229-1924-2

How To Ski & Fix Your Knees

DR. MOIR BOWMAN,
D.C., F.I.A.M.A., DIPL. AC (IAMA)

Chapter 1 Disclaimer: Skiing and in particular skiing in the wilderness is an inherently dangerous activity. This book is not a substitute for going with friends, skiing within your limits, or getting professional instruction. Stay within your limits; the author and publisher are not liable for any damages or negative consequences resulting from the use or misuse of the information provided in this book.

Chapter 2 Disclaimer: The information provided in this book about how to support and heal your knees is for educational and informational purposes only. It is not intended to be a substitute for professional medical advice, diagnosis, or treatment. The author is a licensed chiropractor, but this book does not provide specific medical advice for your situation. It is important that readers seek the advice of a qualified healthcare provider before embarking on any treatment program. The author and publisher are not liable for any damages or negative consequences resulting from the use or misuse of the information provided in this book.

*Dedicated to the Blue-Collar
Working Men and Women*

TABLE OF CONTENTS

INTRODUCTION 1

PART 1 The Ski Resort 43

PART 2 Knees 69

PART 3 77

PART 4 85

EPILOGUE 93

We were mountaineering in the Tetons during the summer. We had left dusty, dry ground. The snow line started at the Meadows campground. We were well above that, on a gigantic snowy slope. I'd never seen anything like it on the east coast. It was a gigantic convex slope. We had been above it for a couple of days during an unsuccessful attempt of the Grand Teton. There were 4 of us; Paul and I, and 2 others who were down either at the Meadows campground or on some other milder objective.

So, we were descending the gigantic snow slope. We weren't wearing crampons but were holding our ice axes in a panicked grip. One could fall and slide 1,000 feet. But in parts there were boulder fields sticking up through the snow. Or fallen giant evergreen trees. It would not do to hit those going 30-mph. My stomach was so upset.

High above one could see birds circling around the blue sky. They weren't stressed. For them, it was nothing. We were operating in a nauseated panic. Or at least I was, as Paul was far more experienced than me.

Then suddenly I heard a whomp, and a stomp; and there was a skier. He was having a great time; he was not only skiing past me, he was kicking and jumping his skis to go faster. There I was at death's grim door and there he was, having the time of his life. He would ski down the slope in 15 minutes that would take us hours. From there, he would hike out the same day, skis attached to his pack. Maybe he had hiking shoes in the small pack on his back.

That's when I knew that becoming proficient in the mountains meant becoming proficient in skiing. It was a decision that made itself. At least for me; my climbing partners were not as convinced.

Upon return to civilization, I planned my foray into skiing: studied the black diamond catalogue; bought a pair of skis described as "being able to do everything". I don't remember the width. And bought at bindings, also from the Black Diamond catalog: the Swiss Diamir-Fritschi binding called "The Scout." They have a ½" by ½" bar that runs along from the heel to the toe piece. The company still produces them and improves them.

That winter, I began to go to a local ski resort. Once with my late brother Mark. He had been skiing before.

I was learning. I remembered seeing him at the bottom of a blue slope. I was sticking to the green (beginner) slopes. He looked as if he'd fallen repeatedly; he was soaked with sweat and snow. His hair was mussed. He looked as if he had taken a beating; I was so proud of him: physical, active, not afraid to take a risk. On that night, I wouldn't have skied a blue slope.

I kept going and eventually moved onto the blue and black slopes. I remember ski lift workers frowning at me disapprovingly upon seeing the AT bindings. The rod under the foot lifts the boots up 1" off the ski. But I paid them no attention and skied fine on the (east coast) black diamonds. After which, they relaxed. I skied with those AT bindings all over the resort. And used big, heavy, downhill boots with them: the only boots I could find that would accommodate my size 15 feet.

After a few years of skiing, a pal Jeff and I went to the Ruth Gorge in Alaska. That would be like playing in the Super Bowl if I had been a football player. One goes to Talkeetna, Alaska; and sits around for a day or 2 waiting for good weather. We stayed in a little wood hotel. I was able to do a little skiing on a local fire road. It's that one buys skins: sticky, long nylon and mohair strips that are adhesive on one side and hairy on the other. And the hairs all go in one direction, so one can walk uphill. The skis won't slide backwards and one can ski downhill, only not as fast as if one removes the skins and slides down on the waxed ski surface: the waxed skis go much faster downhill than if one wears the skins downhill. But it's impossible to walk up any real hill without skins, much less ascend a mountain slope.

In addition to skins, going uphill requires an AT binding. AT might refer to Alpine Touring. It's a ski binding that allows the heel to rise. One could not point skis up a hill if the heel was locked down to the ski. No, the heel must rise upward, the same as in a walking motion. Furthermore, there are little bumps or plastic blocks that fit under the heel to allow the heel to rest upon them even while lifted away from the ski base.

There we were in Talkeetna, whereupon, after a day or 2 of studying the weather, a little airplane took Jeff and I out to the Ruth glacier. The pilot flew a little bit scary, diving near a giant mountain, explaining "it was all part of the experience." We landed on a glacier and stepped out of the cockpit. A man and woman came running up to the plane, all exasperated, "We've been trapped out here 9-days waiting for a plane! Oh, do take us home! I am missing work." Our pilot obliged them and dropped us off with our packs onto the glacier. The pilot directed us to a safe spot to pitch our tents: safe from avalanches. A big hill sat off to the side with a cabin on the top of it. Way off in the middle of the glacier sat a privy. No walls, merely a seat. My 1st act was to dust snow off my skis with my bare hands; and I cut several bleeding slices onto my fingers. So, be aware, the ski edges are super sharp.

It was impossible to walk on the glacier as the snow was too deep. One sinks to the crotch level. It might be possible to make a few inches of progress with each step. Or not. To go anywhere, it was essential to put the skis on. Then it was easy. The glacier was flat there at the landing strip.

With skis we could ambulate. We moved our packs to where the pilot had directed us. Jeff set up his tent and immediately spent a few hours digging a deep, ample snow cave, "In case the weather gets bad; 80mph winds and non-stop blizzards." Years later I still marvel at what a great move that was; although we had mild weather during our trip.

We were given a gigantic, black, heavy radio that I never figured out how to operate. It made squeaking sounds alternating with static sounds.

While I had new Black Diamond skis, downhill boots, bindings, etc., Jeff opted to rent skis. He spent far less than me. To be fair, he struggled with some pliers or a Leatherman tool on the glacier; he was bending or adjusting some infernal metal deficiency on his bindings. It wasn't easy for him. He grimaced and I felt correct about my decision to have arrived with a full contingent of newish equipment.

But Jeff might have had the last laugh. Besides having to rip at his bindings with pliers somewhat regularly throughout the trip, he kept up with me every step of the way. Jeff, well, rented everything. As I said, in the end, years from then, when I went on a 12-year break from climbing due in part to a severe bankruptcy, Jeff was building a fortune. During my bankruptcy time I couldn't imagine taking even a weekend drive to West Virginia for the cost of the gas. But Jeff was building a fortune.

25 years later I would visit Jeff in his home. It was the biggest and most beautiful house I've ever been in. There was a guest house or garage off to the side, which was bigger than any house I've ever been in but paled in comparison with the main house. The house couldn't hold normal furniture. The cabinets had to be 18 feet tall. The furniture had to be so oversized to match the house. One reminisced about *Alice in Wonderland*. That place was as tasteful and enthralling as the host. He was kind and humorous. I felt transported to another world, perhaps one in which I finally achieved all my goals and no longer had any stress.

All I could do in his house was walk around saying, "this place looks like crap!"

Another thing about Jeff was that he objected to our trip being only 5 days. 5 days was all I could fathom. I was so broke. And I chose 5-days thinking that bad weather might extend it to 9-days or 7-days. For which Jeff, although he went along with me and my impoverished mentality, roundly humiliated me by pointing out that "We should be going for at least a week and 2-weeks would be better." He was right about that.

By the time one flies to Alaska, to Anchorage, eats in a restaurant overlooking boats with blue paint peeling from their hulls, and then flies by another plane to be let off on a glacier, yes, 2-weeks makes more sense.

On the other hand, there's nothing wrong with being extremely broke and it was, after all, 5 days on a glacier, in 2 different tents, with just the 2 of us. Perhaps a longer trip would go better, perhaps with a bigger group of friends. Maybe 3 or 4 or 6 different buddies.

So, Jeff was smarter than me as far as saving expenses. My "money is no object" approach was largely or partly responsible for my eventual bankruptcy and 12-year layoff from climbing. Don't hate me, it was a Chapter 13 – I had to pay it all back. Chapter 7's where the debt gets wiped out.

Towards the end of our time on the glacier, we ran into a group of 4 or 5 skiers who weren't experts; but they were friendly. I had run out of whiskey. One of them generously gave me several shots of his whiskey. I remember when he cut me off, 86'd me as it were. But he was right. After the drinks we all went out and tried to ski down a powder mountain slope.

There was an expert there who was skiing down the slope from the summit ridge of that little mountain. He consistently jumped the bergschrund. I tried to ski downhill, same as the other group of 4 or 5 was doing: I failed. I could go 4 or 5 feet before collapsing into the powder. Now, 20 years later, I suspect my skinny skis might have been at least partly responsible.

By the end of that evening, post whiskey and after falling repeatedly into powder snow, I crept into my tent and into my sleeping bag. I was hypothermic; evidenced by that I zipped myself into my expedition −60F sleeping bag. By zipped into, I mean I zipped it all the way closed. The temperature outside was in the 30F's. We slept early. By 1 or 2am, I remember finally feeling warm and partly unzipping the bag. I don't think I ever fully zipped up that bag even during −20F ice climbing trips. But on that night, I was chilled to the bone: highly dangerous. And thank you to the guy who cut me off when he did from further whiskey consumption.

And thanks to him for sharing his whiskey with me, on a remote Alaskan glacier: impressive.

Years later I almost got Jeff to go to New Hampshire with me and I told him to buy ice creepers for our ascent of Mt. Washington. No, so far, I have never summitted it. Jeff never bought the creepers. I bought them and used them once on the sidewalk outside of my house.

I got into sports betting years later and tried unsuccessfully to drag Jeff into that with me. He advised not to do it. I only lost.... not sure, probably less than $1,000 before I realized it was unbeatable. The 10% extra one loses when wrong makes it unbeatable.

I have a friend who made his living betting baseball, but he worked at it 60 or 70-hours weekly. And he has since moved on from that to a paid position high in the sports betting industry.

My point being, Jeff was smart, and mountain climbing's expensive. However, it can be done efficiently and doesn't have to be done the way that I used to do it. Follow Jeff's example, not mine.

The AT Fritsche Scout bindings might be going out of style, but they are easy to step into. They have a jaw clamp at the front and back. If one steps into and out of skis all day long, they will be so easy to use. When I returned to skiing after a 12 year break, I repurchased them. They sat in a room for 6 months before I saw the new style bindings on a website whereupon I returned the Scout bindings.

The Scout bindings are Frame Bindings which mean they lift up with the heel off of the ski: the entire binding lifts up off of the ski. And that's heavy. Also, the toe jaw clamp doesn't match the modern Tech bindings. The pivot point of the scout bindings sits too far in front of the ski boot, and this will tire the skier on a long day. They are being replaced by the Tech bindings: 2 steel cones from the bindings stick into 2 little steel cone shaped holes on the welt of the toe of the ski boot, putting the pivot point at mid toes instead of well in front of the ski boot. But the Scout bindings are still being made and sold. And they are easier to get into than the Tech bindings. I'm ever so slowly getting better with my Tech bindings.

But it's been a process. The first time I took my Tech bindings out was for a stroll around Leesburg, VA during one of our "once a winter snow storms." And mostly it was an exercise in struggling with the binding. The next time I used the Tech binding was in New Hampshire on the Cherbourg trail: it was −1F with a 70mph wind, gusting to 85mph. And my inability to click quickly into the Tech bindings was one factor in my almost not returning from that outing.

I'm not sure why I purchased my skis without any advice from local shops. It's left me with several skis, but still wanting a 95mm ski for the bumpy, slushy manmade snow slopes we have here in the east. Seriously, right from the start, I should have gone with advice from a local ski shop. And they recommend the 95mm skis I now want so I can get down the blue slopes without falling.

And when I finally got help from ski shops in Jasper, Canada; the salesman there explained my true size and the exact boot I needed for Tech boots. Had I started with his advice, I might not have lost my toenails twice. Nor would I be stuck with a pair of extremely expensive, nearly unsellable boots in my closet. The stores are packed with experts; friendly, knowledgeable, humble experts: start there. Go to a person in a store.

If we review my discussion of skiing, it went - I bought skis, bought AT bindings, and then went on the Ruth Gorge, AK trip. The point being that if one positively will have only 1 pair of skis, then go ahead and get AT bindings because you can use those at the ski resort as well as in the backcountry. But after my 12-year layoff, upon re-entry into skiing, I bought a strictly downhill or alpine ski and alpine binding (for use at ski resorts). And then later branched out into the AT binding. Remember the AT bindings require skins;

and if you're going out into the backcountry, you must have an avalanche beacon, a shovel, a probe, probably an airbag, and hopefully 2 or 3 partners.

Back during my 1st effort at skiing, pre-bankruptcy, there were no avalanche airbags. But there was a tube in a vest and that tube was supposed to help one breath if buried in an avalanche. I don't think anyone makes this product anymore. It's been replaced by $1,000 to $1,800 air avalanche bags.

I am no expert. I skied 7 times last winter (flu). And ½ way through this winter, I've been out twice. Let me share my recent 2 ventures into Canadian backcountry.

For some reason we decided to visit the Selkirk mountains in Canada in January 2023. I saw on a website that the Crowfoot Glacier in Alberta, Canada was "a great place to ski on high avalanche danger days." I'd flown into Canada the day before and struck out on the 2d day to the Crowfoot Glacier overlook. There were several cars with skiers standing around parked along the roadside. I walked up and asked, "where do I go and what do I do?" And those skiers gave me the beta about, "Well this whole area's avalanche terrain and one should have a shovel, probe, and beacon to go skiing here," politely leaving off avy air bag which costs over $1,000. But later I saw everyone that day was wearing an avalanche air bag. Everyone there had one.

Perhaps there were 8 skiers standing around there. They were polite and helpful although they were brusque when I explained how I thought this area would be safe from avalanches.

Another skier advised me that "the steepest part's right here off the roadside; beyond that it's milder." Thank you, kind sir, for helpful advice. By the time I got the skins on my skis, got into my boots, and into my pack, assembled my poles, etc., I was the only one on the roadside. Sure enough, there was a steep drop from the road down into the woods. The type of drop that's too steep for me to ski. But expert skiers can fly straight down it. So, I started down the steep slope and immediately my ski came off.

It was the 1st time I'd skied in those skis and ski bindings. It occurred to me that perhaps I'd set the release mechanism too light and that the ski binding might continually release without any pressure on it. And I had no screwdriver to tighten the binding.

So far, I've used the Tecton 12 or Tecton 13 bindings. And for them, as well as for all my downhill (ski resort) bindings, I always put the binding on the lightest possible setting. I've never had any trouble with this. Probably because I have long, tall, extremely skinny legs. The spring-loaded devices and ski manufacturers are calculating release forces based on average legs, ankles, and feet. I'm 6' 5" and have skinny legs. It doesn't mean I can't hike a long way, but I have bird legs. So, my ankles and lower leg bones exert far less force onto my boots and bindings than someone with a thicker or shorter leg.

Anyway, I was initially worried that the bindings were going to release ridiculously easy and that I'd never get the skis to support my weight. Obviously, it wasn't optimal to use the skis and bindings for the 1st time ever on a ski tour alone below the Crowfoot Glacier overlook.

I was extremely much wishing I'd brought a screwdriver to be able to adjust (tighten) the ski bindings. But as it turned out, I merely had clipped into the bindings incorrectly and the lightest setting was completely adequate for my use. But it's worth remembering that perhaps a light screwdriver might be worth taking along.

By the time the ski came off, I was 20-feet down a steep hill in 5-foot-deep snow powder. I'm not sure I'd have been able to walk back up the hill without my skis. And I could not, for all the effort I could muster in this world, get my right boot to click back into the ski binding. Remember the previous winter I'd only been out 7-times and of those times I'd only used the backcountry skis once. And that once was at a resort where the snow gets packed down every night by giant machines.

Here there was no firm surface to stand on; it was deep, loose, unconsolidated snow. After 15-minutes of not being able to get my ski back on, I came up with a plan to hike/wallow down the hill to the flat area at the bottom of the hill. Once there, the terrain leveled out. I was able to get the ski back on. Part of the help was that other skiers had packed snow down a little bit there and I was able to semi-stand on some of the harder snow.

It turns out that the ski came off because I hadn't put it on correctly; it wasn't due to the spring not being tight enough. It turned out that the lightest setting was correct for me. Once I got both skis on, I headed out away from the road, following the skin tracks of the previous skiers.

I feared the ski coming off because I didn't want to spend another 20-minutes putting the ski on again. And the snow was deep and loose and fluffy. If I slipped off the skin track, I fell into the snow and I couldn't get back up. I could but it took a long time and all my strength. I sunk deep into the powdery snow and there was nothing firm to grab onto or push myself up off.

Someone told me years ago to cross my 2 poles into an x and push off that. By the way, even on a packed snow slope at a resort, it's impossible to put the ski back on unless that ski's the uphill ski. If one foot's in the ski binding and the other foot has come out, to put the foot that's out back into the binding, that ski must be on the uphill side. If it's on the downhill side one can never get the ski back onto the boot.

And this applies as well in the backcountry. I followed the skin tracks of the other skiers for an hour or 2. They went out across a lake. I hoped that lake was frozen because falling through the ice would be fatal. But other skiers had gone there and so I followed. But finally, I felt afraid to cut directly across the lake although most of the skiers had done that. Instead, I crept along less used tracks that hugged the shore of the lake.

I was unable to get one of my bindings to go into walk mode. First it was one foot and then it was the other. I couldn't get the heel to rise in walk mode. One foot would but the other foot's heel was locked down onto the ski as if I was ready to ski downhill.

So, I was lumping along with a normal gait on one foot but sliding the other along as best I could while the heel was locked into the ski. I could unhook my boot from the binding, but upon walking again, the boot locked into the heel again. One foot had the heel free to allow for a normal walking gait, while the other foot was locked into the binding.

And the free foot was once my left foot and then later became the right foot. And I bent down low and backwards and pulled upward with great force on the binding but could not lift the gait of the binding up. I pulled hard. I thought of an ancient warrior trying to lift a weapon out of the earth or a rock.

I resolved to ask the next skier I saw, despite the acutely embarrassing nature of the question, "How do I get this binding into walk mode?" And I worried about if I'd be able to get back up the hill since one heel was locked flat into the ski binding. "What if I can't get back up that hill?"

At one point most of the ski trails went across the lake but I, ever cautious, decided to creep along the shore; on the lake but close to the shore. I was afraid of falling in the lake. Once I left the main ski tracks the auxiliary tracks were significantly snowier and less defined. And I began to lose my footing; the skis would slide off the track and I'd fall. I could plunge the ski pole into the soft snow about 2 or 3 feet before it would hit the frozen ice of the pond surface. Whereas back on the main ski track, the poles were hitting into tough icy snow on either side of the tracks.

Finally, I came to a deadfall which enabled me to sit down sideways onto the fallen tree without having to remove the skis. I felt I might not be able to get the skis back on again; or if I did, that it would take 25 minutes. I rested for a while on the deadfall. It got cold. Previously I'd been sweating in my 1-piece ski suit with multiple layers of clothing underneath. But once I stopped, it got cold, scaring me.

About 1/2 mile off, on the other side of the lake, I saw 3 figures, 3-backcountry skiers. They had taken the circuitous route that I was on although they were far ahead of me.

In retrospect, I should have removed my skins once I got onto the flat lake. I could have glided along so much more quickly.

I was unable to rest for 1 hour because it was too cold. And I was worried about getting up the hill and whether the skis would function normally. By the time I headed back, I don't know how, but I'd gotten both skis to operate in walk mode.

I followed the ski tracks back the way I came and soon became confused as to where I'd come from. Someone familiar with those mountains wouldn't have gotten lost, but I hadn't examined the mountain surroundings because I'd been so busy fighting the bindings. There were many trails going in different directions. No skiers were visible. It was daytime but so dark, cloudy, and cold.

As it turned out, although I thought I had packed my GPS unit, I hadn't. I remembered having checked off on my list that I had it. Later at home I'd find that I hadn't checked off GPS but had put a question mark next to that item. I incorrectly remembered having taken the batteries out of the unit to put in fresh batteries. None of that had happened. The GPS unit can show me, if I have glasses on, where I'd come from.

But I picked the correct trails and experienced relief upon regaining the flatter more used ski tracks. At least initially, but as time wore on, I became lost and confused about which ski tracks were going where. All of this was on a lake. Probably the local skiers knew the lake was rock solid safe to ski on. But I didn't. The through of breaking through into that dark freezing water was unpleasant.

Where I was lost, local skiers would easily navigate their way back to the car or out to whatever ski run they were seeking. As a man who had a beer with me in a bar later that week explained, "the scale of the mountains out here is so big that it's impossible to get lost." He was referring to, long ago, when he had summited

2 of the biggest mountains in the range. He had slept in snow caves. He and his partner had 6mm rope for crevasse rescue.

Probably if I knew the mountains, I wouldn't have felt lost. But I had gone out from the car mostly focused head down on my bindings. I only glanced around at the mountains once I realized I was lost. And I sort of imagined the way back to the car must be "over there." And it was. But it was quite traumatic to realize that I didn't know for sure: on the gloomy, dark, cold day. In thick powder. And somehow the parties that had left ahead of me were no longer visible or audible.

That was one of those moments that, upon my return to Virginia, caused me "to take a moment." It gave me post-traumatic stress disorder. But on that day, I blundered along into the pines and found the correct tracks and returned the correct way.

When I got to the hill that I had been so worried about, I surmounted that with ease. The skins worked great. By then I was heel free on both skis. That was a fun little diversion.

I returned to the hotel room. That night I watched a YouTube video about how to operate the bindings. One merely pulls up on the rear handle but while the heel of the boot is not sitting in the bindings. Those are some tough bindings, and I was fortunate not to have broken them.

Once I returned home, I found the GPS unit (along with my compass) sitting in a hiking pack.

I've put all the electronics into one pouch inside the avalanche air bag pack "the avy pack": the GPS unit, the avalanche beacon, the Garmin in Reach device, and the compass. There are too many little items to remember so, I'll keep them together in a bag. Hopefully I'll put some powerful reading glasses in the case as well because none of those items will work if I don't have my glasses.

And promised myself for the 3 millionth time that I'd go to the US Geological Survey building in Reston and buy topo maps and practice with the GPS unit. I've used it for 20 years but never figured out how to pinpoint exactly where I am on a map. It can be done. But even without that ability, if I have glasses, the GPS can show the direction of a starting point provided I marked the point at the start of the journey.

I knew when I started that day that I didn't have the GPS with me. But I thought I'd be able to ski around the same area in a safe manner without losing my bearings. And I wasn't totally turned around, but I was confused enough that the experience was traumatic. I wouldn't have wanted to get stuck out in that cold on a frozen lake. I don't know if I'd have remembered that I had the Garmin in reach device with me. I certainly wouldn't have wanted to call for a satellite rescue. It would beat freezing to death, but not by much.

I also regretted that I hadn't followed my rule last winter – (flu) about clicking into and out of the ski bindings at least 100 times in the house to familiarize myself to that process; and to set off and repack the air back twice each ski season.

I didn't tighten my Scarpa Maestrale boots much and found, same as 2 seasons ago, that I had bloodied the base of my big left toenail. I will now lose the nail over a several week period. Later in the trip I went to a store where a sales manager pointed out to me that the Scarpas have (I remembered seeing it myself once he explained it) 3 empty bolt holes to shift the tightening latches to make the boot tighter.

And the salesman warned me against putting the flaps of the boot on incorrectly lest I break the plastic. I have always put the flaps on incorrectly and did so on the lake. The plastic's a little warped and bent. Of course, this was at 5:50pm and the store closed at 6pm. I searched for the little boot wrenches to modify the latch placement myself but had left the wrenches at home. I remembered thinking, "Nah, I won't need these; these boots are fine."

That meant I had to wait until the next morning at 10am for the shop to open. The manager moved the buckles with an Allen wrench device at no charge for me the next morning. He was so kind. Which made me more embarrassed about having torqued my boots shut with the flaps incorrectly placed. Think, for example, of tying tennis shoes but with the tongue of the shoe sticking out on one side.

Now I have it figured out but might forget by next winter. I explained to the manager, "I'm terrible at every aspect of the sport – ice climbing, rock climbing, skiing, etc. But I practice every aspect of the sport." And he was pleased upon hearing that from me. I no longer felt ashamed.

By the way, waiting until 10am the next day effectively ended for that day – my last day- any chance I had of going skiing. Maybe it was for the best as I was severely exhausted upon my return home after the vacation.

I didn't want to ski on bloody big toenails; well, I would have until I heard the boots could be corrected. Once I heard that I decided to forget skiing on the loose boots and get them fixed.

To be clear, I met the 2d ski manager after my 2d day of skiing.

We might categorize my adventure near the Crowfoot Glacier as type 2 fun: it wasn't fun while I was experiencing it; but it became fun later once I was back in civilization and remembered the scenery, the view of the glaciers, and the daunting Canadian mountains and pines all around.

Now, sitting in my e-z chair, the memory of those dark could mountains fills me with peace. I want to go back and reach the ski slopes the other skiers had gone to. Remember in my story, I had only skied upon the flat lake, and only gotten about 1/3 of the way around the lake. Across the lake were hills and mountains where the other skiers were headed to skin up and then ski down.

In 1 store in Jasper a manager measured my feet in a shoe tree which had an electrostatic sheet and he promised me that I was a true 31.5. The Scarpas were a 32.5 and cavernous compared to my feet. The manager suggested, as an emergency measure, I might try wearing double socks. At the time of that fitting, I was in post-traumatic shock and somehow convinced that my boots were too short.

The manager advised me to switch to a 31.5 Salomon boot which would be skinnier and had 4 secure buckles and an improved switch for switching between walk and run mode. Only several days later did I stop panicking enough to consider that the ski boot manager might know what he was talking about.

I found a pair of 31.5 Salomon boots and used them at a ski resort. They fit perfectly, but I must use them in the mountains to know for sure they are correct for my feet.

When the ski manager initially measured my feet, he informed me I was a 31.5, but they didn't have that size in the store. Here my thinking was not too clear: I thought he merely wanted to sell me a boot and chose the 31.5 size arbitrarily since that was the only size they'd be able to sell me. I was paranoid and not thinking clearly. And by the next day when a different store pointed out that my 32.5 Scarpas could be modified, I become more convinced the 1st ski manager wasn't being truthful with me.

As time has gone on, it's become clear that the ski store manager (1) took the time to carefully measure my feet on a sophisticated sizing device; and (2) he was utterly selfless and helpful to me. I found the 31.5 Salomon boots he recommended: also, as he pointed out, those boots can be heated in an oven and sized for my feet.

I was paranoid and negative because I was suffering from post-traumatic stress from my experiences in the backcountry. It's hard to convey here the pressure I felt worrying about not being able to get back to the car; 1st at Crowfoot Glacier when I didn't know if my bindings would work, if I could get back up the hill with my heels locked into the bindings, and if I could find the correct path back to the parking area.

I've lost my way 1 hour from my car here locally on the Appalachian Trail in Virginia, on a trail I've hiked a dozen times. There was a shelter I hadn't seen, a signpost with directions that were useless, a parking lot I'd never seen, hunting stands in trees as I blundered along private property, etc. Finally, I headed off in a certain direction on pure intuition and it worked out fine. My point being fatigue and stress in the mountains aggressively confuse one's thinking. And the fear, the consequences of how bad things can go if they do go bad, that pressure builds and causes a bruise in the mind of a vulnerable skier or hiker.

My 2d outing was to the Balds at Maligne lake. During the ascent of the trail there I worried that I wouldn't be able to ski successfully down the fire road. What would happen if I had to hike down? How long would it take? What if I fell hard and broke a bone? What if the snow proved too soft for hiking without my skis? And in each place, it was cold during the

10-minute breaks: what would happen if I had to spend overnight outside?

This pressure, at once alluring and horrible, builds relentlessly as the hours roll by. And it's not that my situation was world class dangerous: local Canadians would view the same position as purely enjoyable, simply a walk in the park, all in a day's adventure. On the other hand, I've been visiting the mountains for most of my life, I train hard for a non-professional athlete, and I'm more skilled in the mountains than the average person.

But the fear and dread that built up in my brain spilled out into unclear thinking about the salesman's clear-headed advice. Also, I had bloodied and damaged the toenails on my feet. That's an injury. That pushed my sense of dread and worry about whether I'd be able to continue pursuing backcountry skiing. There's something about getting hurt, about things going wrong, when no one's around except small dark squirrels and deep white snow.

I'm not proud of my paranoia and bad feelings towards the expert sales manager but wanted to share them as an example of what the brain will do under pressure in the wilderness; how that stress will warp one's thinking for several days after surviving the experience.

2 seasons prior I took my new Tech bindings and skis out to Mt. Washington. We had a week in North Conway, and I thought I'd head up to the famous Pinnacle gully and so forth. I awoke at 2am, packed up, and headed to the parking lot on Mt. Washington. I decided to go up the path to Mt. Washington and ski down the Cherbourg fire trail. I hadn't been out in real winter in a while and seriously underestimated the cold of Mt. Washington.

I had a puffy jacket and pants in my avy pack. But the pants I wore that day were lightweight Long Johns covered by a lightweight stretch activist pant. I estimated that hiking up the hill would be hot work and it was. But the 10-minute breaks were chilly and as the day wore on, I became seriously cold.

I struggled with the small metallic buckle on the avy pack (1st time using the pack). My hat (gorilla balaclava) was mercifully windproof but kept twisting around my head and limiting my vision. On the way up the trail I took a guess at a non-descript fork in the trail and was luckily correct. A family of a dad, his wife, a maybe 30-year-old son, and a little girl passed me. And then I passed them. And then I got ahead of them. But not before I teased the 30'ish year-old young man about "I'll see him up top unless you get scared."

"I'll be there," he replied grimly. Near the top of the trail, I was passed by many jovial college aged young men. Also, there was a young couple heading up with full packs obviously preparing to overnight. Yes, I can camp in those conditions (see my sleeping bag rated to –60F under my bed). But it was impressive to see them. Temperatures were about –1F and there was 60mph wind whipping about, especially as we got higher up the mountain.

I was struggling terribly with the Tech bindings: the effort of getting the 2 little metal horns to go into the 2 little cones on the toe of the ski boot was extremely difficult. During my short breaks I froze. My GU – the large 15 serving size – was too cold to squeeze out of the container. It was as if I was too cold to stop and put on my coat and warm pants. I don't know why I didn't think to do that.

Finally at the top of the trail things began to fall apart. There was a big, closed cabin with a porch where 6 or so skiers were taking a break. I didn't go onto the porch because I didn't know if I could get my skis back on if I took them off. So, I lay down in the snow 20-feet away from the porch. The wind was kicking up to more than 60mph and blowing snow with it. During my 10-minute break, the young skiers got off the porch, clipped into their skis and passed me.

They asked if I was ok, and I gave them the big thumbs up gesture. I was so like the doctor in the movie Everest who was sitting there, immobile, not appreciating the peril he was in. It was a dangerous situation. The young skiers disappeared expertly down the Cherbourg fire road. When I rose from laying down (so as to keep attached to my skis), I locked in my heels for the descent and pointed my skis downward to drop in onto the Cherbourg fire road.

There was a little creek with running water which I tried to avoid but got the skis partially into. And then the water on the bottom of the skis made a thick snowy crust form on the bottom of the skis. I couldn't glide at all. I tried scraping the edge of one ski against the bottom of the other. Finally, I rubbed the bottom of the skis against some pine trees and removed the snowy crust that had formed on the bottom.

I frequently removed my gloves trying to clip the boots into the bindings, trying to get the heel clip into the proper position for either walking or skiing, etc. The little words "walk, ski, enter" on the bindings were obscured by snow. My pants kept slipping down; I had forgotten how to operate the simple toggle clasp to hold them up and I couldn't see it easily for the goggles, jacket, hip belt of the pack, etc. Finally, I began to descend Cherbourg Road. I tried to go slow, but the road was too steep. 80mph wind gusts push me from behind, shoving me down the slope. I flew off the road into trees. A ski came off. One foot plunged into 4 feet of powder snow while the other foot was standing on hard ice. Again, I got my gloves off to help me get back into the bindings.

I couldn't ski down the road as it was too steep. I would fly out of control each time I went down it. As a salesman in town later explained, "Skiing black diamond at a resort means nothing out on the fire road." I'd intentionally fall once I got out of control so as not to keep accelerating and experience an ever harder out of control fall. During the falls I'd lose a ski and spend so long trying to get it back on.

Finally, after an hour or more, I gave up on skiing down the road and took my skis off. The avy pack had a carry system for the skis so I didn't have to carry them. I had tightened my left boot but due to the stress and wind and cold I never quite got around to tightening the right boot. I didn't have ice creepers or crampons and it was a challenge hiking down the sometimes super icy and sometimes super deep snowy road. A long time went by.

The worst nightmare of all came when, sure enough, here came the family I'd passed skinning up the trail. First was the little girl, then the dad who so kindly told me, "It was the worst conditions I'd ever seen"; then the mom and finally the son who grimly skied by me. They were skiing well, in control, enjoying the turns, happy as clams; and there I was, hiking down with my skis attached to my pack.

It never occurred to me to put on my warm pants. Somehow the effort of removing my pack, of stopping, of unzipping something was too much to consider. Another hour went by. Here came 2 more skiers; I still remember the one guy, his skis skidding expertly sideways on the ice, him and his buddy enjoying their descent.

Eventually, mercifully, I saw 2 hikers off to the skier's left (i.e., the left side if one was facing downhill) of the road. They were ice climbers returning from a day out on the gullies up on Mt. Washington. And I went to where they had been; I mean, I got off the horrible fire road and onto a trail that was walkable. At this point I felt so much safer. I had not realized there were trails off to the left of the road. I put on my warm jacket.

I began to see trail signs indicating I was approaching the parking area. I was so extremely happy. I joked manically with any hiker going uphill past me. The footing was far superior to what I had endured on the Cherbourg Road. I was, after all, on a trail I knew, headed back to the parking lot. I passed a group of high school boys who were hiking up the trail and advised one to "zip up your jacket: the wind's blowing up there." I arrived back at the parking lot.

A 70mph gust of wind blasted me as I took off my skis. I unpacked, unclipped, and shoved everything in the car.

Back in the hotel room I saw I had ruined my large right toenail: it was black (the boot I hadn't tightened – it felt comfortable at the time). And due to the many rough tumbles I had taken, my fingers were numb. It was a good thing I'm a chiropractor to understand that bouncing my neck during falls was responsible for the numbness in my fingertips. And yet, as time wore on, they stayed quite numb: the fingers on both hands felt odd and almost completely numb.

By the next day I realized that my fingers had gotten frostbitten. They stayed numb. I worked all the next week with numb fingers. Patients would say, "It hurts right here," and I'd push on a spot and say, "Oh yes, right there."

"No, not there, over here, the giant muscle spasm."

"Oh right, right," I'd say, "I feel it." And they'd look at me askance, "No, not there, over here, right here." I couldn't feel anything with my fingers. After about a week, all the skin peeled off my fingers. The skin was dry and hard when it peeled off. After all the skin peeled away, normal sensation returned to my fingers.

I had post-traumatic stress syndrome. I sold the boots that had so savaged my toenail. I photographed the boots right in the hotel room and put them on eBay. I sold them for almost nothing. As I recovered from the stress, I tried to get them back. I called the guy who bought the boots, but he had "bought them for his son who really wants them." I merely hinted around about the boots. They were gone.

Eventually I repurchased the same boots, at full price, but couldn't get the best version of the boots but rather a slightly lighter, cheaper version of the boots. Life went on. I recovered.

And so, here I was, 2 years later, in Canada, once again realizing that these boots were not going to work out for my feet. I worried I'd have to switch out boots and Tech bindings and use the old system I had used before, of downhill ski boots with Scout bindings.

But the Scout bindings are going out of fashion: (mentioned earlier in this article). They have a weight problem, and the entire binding lifts with each step, adding weight to the motion of walking. And, of course, I would wear gigantic clunky downhill boots with them. But I never bloodied or lost my toenails with that set up. And so what if it's heavy: my big thigh muscles can handle it. So, it's a work in progress.

Worst case I can still go backcountry skiing even if I must give up on the sleek looking Tech hybrid bindings. They are hard to step into. The Scout bindings lock in with a jaw on the heel and the toe and they are so much easier to get into than the Tech bindings and their 2 steel pins. Currently it seems as though the new Salomon boots will work well, and I can use the modern Tech bindings. Update: the Salomon boots work great during a long day at the resort while the Scarpa boots rely too much on the ankle straps and not enough on the entire boot packing up against my ankles and feet: they cannot protect my toes from hitting against the front of the boot, even with the buckles moved to their tightest position. Remember, I have long skinny feet and skinny legs.

Prior to my visits to the ski shops in Jasper I had gone on a 2d day of skiing. During the 2d day of skiing I tightened all the buckles down to either their tightest level or nearly the tightest level. At the end of that much longer day I still hurt both toenails on my big toes. The right one was hurt after the 2d day although I hadn't noticed any injury to it after the 1st day. This occurred 2 seasons ago also, in New Hampshire, but only to the boot I had failed to tighten.

After that New Hampshire trip I returned home and made so many phone calls including to expert east coast boot fitters: they can be found at big ski resorts. They were generous with their time and advice to me over the phone. Finally, there in the hotel in Banff, it occurred to me to go to local stores for help; to get examined by sales managers/boot fitters in person. And those guys were super smart. I will buy equipment from their stores and tell the store owners about the exemplary attitude of those helpful sales managers.

I went to the web where a salesman found the 31.5 Salomon boots for me. I never could have found them on the web myself.

I went on the web because it's so easy to return things and I worried the Salomon boots would be too small. That and I hate asking a brick-and-mortar store "can you match the price of the internet?" I figured the Canadian stores wouldn't be able to, and if they did, I'd be so embarrassed to return the boots to them, all by international mail. I don't feel great about it. I owe those managers in Jasper for their attention, expertise, and kindness. But I will keep a sharp eye for all future purchases; eventually the web will falter on something and then I'll order from the stores in Jasper. As they say, mountain climbing's expensive. I won't let those guys down.

Time will tell which systems will work for my enormous size 15 feet. All you normal foot sized people, count your blessings. Be grateful for the indignity and pain you will be spared.

The 2d trip during that January 2023 Banff vacation:

A helper at a local store told me many touring areas were closed because of "people protesting over protecting caribou habitat but the Balds at Maligne Lake were open for backcountry skiing."

I bumbled into a man walking along the street 5 minutes later who told me the same thing. That settled it.

The next morning, I took off for the Balds. I had a late start aggravated by stopping for gas and later by realizing I had left my gloves back in the hotel room. I was driving along when suddenly I had a funny feeling, such as, "Wait, where are my gloves?" I did a U-turn and headed back to the hotel. Once there I found the gloves as well as my big thick wool socks; the only socks besides the little cotton white socks I was wearing. I couldn't have skied that day without gloves or without ski socks.

Then, I headed back to the Balds. And the drive took over an hour. Perhaps it was 1 ½ hours. Finally, I saw a ranger with a camera near the parking area and he explained that "the parking area is on the left and the trail is on the right."

I was so grateful for his advice. It was as he said: I pulled into the parking lot on the left. There was another car and man waiting there: a backcountry skier waiting for his buddy.

The 1st thing to do was to sell 1 of our 2 urinal cakes and get access to the gas station during our stay. (Sleep induced sentence fragment – not edited).

The other 1st thing to do was remove my 1-piece suit and put on the insulated pants under the suit, and then replace the suit; because it felt piercingly cold. I carried the belay parka in the avy pack.

Finally, I was ready and headed off, up the trail. I had a big, bruised, bloody left big toenail damaged on my left foot from not tightening my boots on the Crowfoot Glacier. So, this time, I carefully sinched up both boots as tight as they would go.

The other skier in the parking lot had waited for his buddy who eventually arrived, and they both headed up the trail together 15 minutes before me. I was getting ready as quickly as I could, but it wasn't very fast.

By this time, I had the skis and bindings better dialed, having watched a YouTube video about how to move the binding into walk mode.

I started trudging up the trail. It was a fire road, and the entire fire road was frozen so, I had a platform where I could sit and rest and then stand up on, unlike the loose unconsolidated snow on the Crowfoot Glacier trail.

A few hours passed and I began to overheat inside my clothes and 1 piece suit. I felt trickles of sweat running down my ribs. I began to take longer breaks to cool down. I couldn't sit for long before it became too cold. After 3 hours I came to an official shortcut: it had a sign. I went 20 minutes beyond the shortcut and thought to turn back. I was trying to make a 5-hour day of it as I had a hungry companion waiting for lunch back in the hotel.

I wasn't far off a 5-hour day, but also had the late start, and the 1.5 hour drive each way; I got back well after lunch. That's another story.

I did well to turn back when I did. I didn't know if I could ski back down, or if I'd have to sidestep back down, wear my skins down, or take my skis off entirely and walk back down. Either of the latter 3 options would put me back to the car well after an 8-hour day. But I was able to ski back the whole way. What happened was that there was powder off the sides of the fire road. So, I put one ski into the powder for the slowing effect of it; and put the other ski into sideways braking mode. It took effort. It wasn't easy. But I was able to ski down the entire road doing that. The road was too steep to "pizza brake" the whole way down, and too narrow to allow for skiing from one side to the other. But the powder on the edges of the fire road slowed my ski.

I thoroughly enjoyed skiing down the fire road. It was the closest I've come to backcountry skiing down a mountain. I never reached the Balds; which I assume are treeless tops of the mountain which might afford downhill skiing, especially during less avalanche-prone conditions than we had that day.

The 1.5-hour drive felt as if it took forever to return to the hotel. My hungry companion inside the room wouldn't open the door and my key card had expired.

I noticed both toenails were now damaged and bruised. That was sad as I had tightened the boots fully and believed the fit was correct. It was obvious I was going to lose 1 and probably both big toenails. That afternoon I left the room and headed out to ski stores to beg for some expert attention to my ski boot dilemma. I was upset but it occurred to me to show my feet to locals in jasper who might be able to advise me.

As for now, back home, I've soaked my feet in hot salty water for 20 minutes to try to get the dead toenails to come off. I suspect the right big nail will come off as well, but I am not positive. The ski manager was the only ski expert in this world who was willing to look at my 64-year-old, mangled, size 15 feet. He mentioned the left nail would come off for sure, and maybe the right nail. I suffered this same injury 2 years ago from the same boots. I was going to see a dermatologist to have my dead nail removed. I imagined a $600 bill for that. One of my Latina helpers said to stick my foot in hot water instead. I did that and the dead nail came right off. I'm trying that now but much earlier on in the process.

2 years ago, the nail slowly regrew in a miracle of tissue regeneration. I hope that happens again. But first to remove the dead nails.

We've covered the topic of backcountry skiing almost exclusively so far. But mostly I ski at the local downhill ski resorts. We have 2 or 3 resorts either 1 or 1 ½ hours north of Northern Virginia, across the state line in Pennsylvania.

When one goes there, witness the presence of high school kids who live 15 minutes from the resort and who ski every day. They are skillful. I am not. I am slow. But make no mistake about it, those resorts are thrilling, exciting, dramatic and highly efficient places to train to ski. They have steep runs, moderate runs, nighttime skiing, and allow skiing during times where our Northern Virginia region sits in warm, sunny conditions.

Upon my return to skiing after the 12-year break, I purchased downhill boots, bindings, and skis. And I've been hitting the downhill resorts and learning for the last 6 seasons. I only got into the backcountry misadventures during the last 3 seasons.

It's hard to explain how little downhill skiing prepares one for backcountry skiing. One would expect that there might be some minor glitches upon transitioning from one to the other. No such luck. It's extremely different.

Starting out? Hit the resorts. I can ski black and double black diamonds at the east coast resorts. For a long time, I was the slowest skier on the slope. Maybe once or twice a season I'd get down a slope faster than someone else: some stout little old person. Otherwise, everyone rained past me.

But that didn't take away from the adventure and excitement of the downhill resorts. It's a blast to sit in the ski lift and get wheeled silently up the mountain, to tighten the boots, and to swerve one's way down a packed snow slope 100 to 200 feet wide. So people were racing by me on all sides; so what.

Part 1

❖

THE SKI RESORT

It might be easy to grumble about the crowded resorts, and how ethereal backcountry skiing beats resort or downhill skiing. But they are both wonderful. One could be a resort skier only for their entire career and lead a wonderful life for it.

I've backcountry skied a handful of times compared to many more times spent at the downhill resort: "the frontside skier: a person who skis on the busy, well-skied and groomed steeps." Machines at night pack the snow. If one arrives early, the snow surface will have a hard, smooth surface with a corduroy pattern to it: it's beautiful and fun to ski. As the day wears on, and hundreds of skiers plow across the slope, the snow will become broken, crusty, and rough.

Frontside skiing means when one rides a ski lift to the top and then skis down the front or back of a mountain; usually there's a lodge or shopping center sized buildings at the bottom. There are teams of kids out for the day: squads of red-jacketed rescue/guide personnel swarming over the slopes; families; groups consisting of experts and their out-of-control friends trying to keep up even though it's their 1st day ever skiing. Snowboarders mix with skiers: mom and dad with accomplished athletes.

I don't know why, but until recently I was always the slowest person down the slope. It might be my weight (210 lbs), or my age (64), or maybe because I have long skinny legs. But I go slowly. I can ski east coast double black diamond comfortably, but slowly, ever so slowly. And this colors my experience on groomed slopes. Because I was the slowest skier there, everyone went whizzing past me. For a long time, I didn't ski straight down the mountain but went all the way from one side of the slope to the other. And at each end, before I turned back to go the other direction, I'd look up the slope hoping to avoid skiers speeding down the slopes. Many of them are going quite fast; some are in control, and some aren't.

It sounds as if I'm the one at fault; after all, I am not going with the flow of traffic – I am going significantly slower. So, my strategy and experience on the slopes will be different that others reading this.

But it doesn't take away from the fun of the ski resorts. I love it. And sometimes, near the run out bottom part, I can go straight and extremely fast. Always wear a helmet. Always keep one's goggles on. Get high quality ski gloves: no, a little better than that: I use Black Diamond Enforcer gloves: same pair for 6 years. Once the hands get wet it's impossible to get them into cheap gloves. The enforcer gloves have thick leather palms and padding on the back and fingers to protect the hand during falls. I can usually slide my crippled hands into them when wet or dry, and they are warm.

I found my boot size by going to different stores feigning interest in buying boots, and then ordered them online. That worked for the frontside ski boots but was disastrous for purchasing my skis. Only now, 6 long seasons into skiing, have I realized I purchased the wrong skis. My 69mm skis are great for corduroy condition that exist during the 1st hour of the day, but they are not suitable for the chunky, lumpy, undulating blue slopes with heavy man-made snow. I can ski on bare ice black diamond slopes only to fall repeatedly on bumpy blue slopes. Only now I listened to a local ski shop who advised me to get 95mm wide skis: 6-years of falling. Go to a local ski shop; don't buy your 1st skis alone with no advice.

I lucked out on the boots and have always been comfortable and uninjured in them. I wear orthotics in the ski boots: do that: see a chiropractor and get orthotics by Foot Levelers. Wear thick wool socks inside the boots.

I wore a 1-piece suit last time out but was the only one at the resort in such a suit. Everyone else wore a jacket and ski pants. I threw out my ski pants recently, mistakenly forgetting that I was using them as ski pants. One must have ski pants: a tough nylon shell, pertex or gortex or some such material. Don't pay the rip off prices for new brand name ski pants. At least get something on sale. Jeans won't do, the $30 snow pants at Costco won't do.

Good ski pants will protect the legs from wind, falls onto snow, and from rain. I wear either a 1-piece suit; or insulated pants under the activist tights.

I got cheap aluminum poles and bent one and always rest easy when I leave them unattended while I take a rest or lunch break. The skis might or might not need to be locked up. I locked mine last time out but suspect I was the only one in the resort who had bothered to do so. Where else can one leave a $900 piece of equipment unattended for hours and no one will take it?

The resort's a whole scene: eat lunch there: observe the new families, groups of kids, and everything in between.

Frontside skiing doesn't carry the risk of avalanche. Mostly not the risk of getting lost, at least in east coast resorts. It's more of a fun day and less of a grim day. As the hours wear on, I enjoy sitting on the lift with other skiers. Sometimes I meet someone whose dad I went to high school with. Sometimes I learn from ski instructors spewing their wisdom.

It's eerie to ride noiselessly up steep mountains on silent, thick, safe cables. After spending a lifetime hiking up hills; and suddenly it's all done by sitting in a chair zooming upwards. Initially I was stunned by how daring jumping onto and off the lift was. And then there was a season where I struggled with it when there were others on the chair (because I was allowing myself to be the last to sit down into the chair or the last the leave the chair – avoid that). It happened yesterday: 2 skiers exited the chair before me, and this caused the chair to swing sideways. By the time I exit I'm thrown sideways and end up falling violently onto the snow. It's embarrassing.

But except for yesterday at the start, lately I hardly notice boarding or exiting chair lifts. "Don't ever race the chair;" meaning, if it's moving quickly, simply wait, let it pass, and grab the next chair. I don't know why I was leaving the chair late for the 1st few seasons: was I being polite, timid, passive, or counting on my coordination to allow others to act first? But it led to tumbles and spills. Now intentionally leave either first or simultaneously with the other passengers.

Ditto for sitting onto the chair. I caused so many spills and shuffles and mishaps being the last to sit down on a moving chair that already had 3 recent passengers. So, sit promptly into the chair. Don't let others sit 1st and then expect to compensate.

One can learn so much sitting in the lift. One runs into people who can answer questions or resolve problems. Urgent questions about skiing may be pried out of a captive audience. It's a good time to eat a GU. I break 10 minutes every hour, on the hour, during sports. Riding the chair lift up the mountain does not count as part of the 10-minute break. That break must be taken sitting down in a chair on the ground.

Frontside skiing can be magical. Take the lunch break inside. If one feels too hot, disrobe enough to feel comfortable. Don't sit outside in the wind and cold for an hour: it's harder on the body than it looks.

I've had people fuss at me for sitting (10-minute break) at their table. I've scraped ski poles with out-of-control skiers descending from above and almost hitting me.

Once, before I developed the habit of scanning up-slope before each turn across the slopes, a petit Asian snowboarder hit me hard. She was so polite. I went to go on my way but found she had knocked me out of both skis. She stayed there, friendly, until I reassembled my skis and my wits. She had hit me on the side of my thigh, well above the knee, where I'm strong. No harm done. Worth it. That was the end of me skiing slowly down the slope without searching intently uphill for skiers to avoid.

Sometimes there are scads of skiers speeding by me, so many that I stop moving and let them pass. It's common for some couples to pass me, stop to rest or talk until I pass them, and then descend and pass me again repeatedly all the way down the slope.

Some speed skiers hang tightly to the extreme right or left edge of the slope, so don't think one's safe simply by skiing along the edge of the slope.

Sometimes at night, in the electric light, one skis down a slope into mist churned out by snow blowing machines.

I ski 50 minutes and break 10 minutes. Except for lunch: that's an hour. After getting ill last season, I noticed sitting outside during the lunch break preceded an illness. Therefore, I made a rule about it:

1, take lunch inside, not outside in the wind and cold.

2, don't ski with water balloon gloves. On a rainy day, the gloves can fill with water. Don't allow that: use a shell (one arrives tomorrow – 1st I've owned). If the shell doesn't work, I'll carry a 2d pair of gloves or mitts inside a plastic bag, inside the jacket.

During 10-minute rest breaks, years ago, on the backside of a local resort, they had a wood fire in a fire pit. Next to the fire, speakers played classic rock songs. That was supreme. And if it was snowing, it was doubly supreme: moto benni. But in later years I haven't seen the wood fire: COVID and the inevitable, "well it was too much work anyway so now we'll stop doing that even though there's no more COVID around."

Pre COVID, there were giant stations where eager helpers checked one's skis. For some reason these were eliminated during the COVID scare and they never returned. After all, someone must pay the helpers to stand there and collect skis.

Even without that rare wood fire, there might be gas fire pits around, screened off in front of wooden chairs. Always sit there. Unless there aren't chairs available and then go sit glumly at a picnic table.

I bought skinny skis (70mm at the waist). They ski great down black diamond brown sheets of ice but struggle on clumpy, 7 inch deep, heavy snow found on blues. They work great on corduroy.

When I first returned to skiing, I believed that the Virginia east coast conditions were so pathetic as to allow only the poorest snow conditions. That's been true. I bought the 70mm skis in an attitude of, "well there's never going to be any powder, so let's admit it and stick to skinny skis because that's all we'll need anyway. Let's be honest. And let all the other fools go for the fatter skis in a politically correct but ultimately unrealistic hunt for powdery snow conditions." One web site jokingly referred to these skis as politically incorrect. I won't repeat the full title given.

The problem has become, and it's taken 6 years to realize it, these skinny 70mm skis are awesome on (east coast) double black diamonds which are too steep to allow any accumulation of snow. Brown, icy, steep, stripped slopes are easy in these skis. The problem lies in the blue slopes, especially blue slopes with bumpy terrain. There, a thick gravely compound of manmade snow gathers and, well; it's not powder, but a little wider ski would be so much better than the skinny skis.

Of course, the 70mm (at the waist) Quattro skis work great at first tracks: temperatures below freezing, at the top of a giant run, and all the surface of the snow is corduroy. There's no need for floatation. It's pure edging all the way down to the bottom.

For the thick, clumpy snow found on the less steep blue runs, I've been told to go for about 95mm wide. One salesman said 95mm for our local resorts which have thick, clumpy snow. An out west salesman said 95mm to 100mm. Perhaps by next season I'll try that width out. Meaning maybe I'll get that width ski next August. If I do, I'll order it from the store in Jasper where the salesman helped me out and measured my feet.

On my lone foray out to the Jackson Hole ski resort in Wyoming, a ski expert mentioned, "use skinny skis in the morning and shift over to fatter skis once the slopes have become broken up and warmer." That was good advice. My fatter option is the 106mm Cochise skis.

1 nearby local resort has 3 intense mogul slopes. I can't ski them as the experts do: swishing gracefully amongst the bumps, curving around the gigantic pillars all sinewy and in control. But I can descend the slopes in one desperate sideways motion after another. Stopping and panting at the edge of the run, turning around and barely managing to scratch my way to the other side. For these mogul runs I got, predictably, even skinnier, super short, "2020 Hart F17 Fusion World Class Mogul skis."

I can ski all over the resort on these short little skis. On a gigantic green or blue corduroy hill, they tire me out a little bit because of their small braking surface. A full-length ski with its full-length brakes (edges) makes for more comfortable skiing. But sure enough, in the gigantic ridiculously aggressive moguls, the little mogul skis work best.

I have 2 longest length skis and the shortest length mogul skis. Note that professional mogul skiers might choose the mogul skis in the longest length. I can't figure that out yet. Maybe one day.

So, the longer skis offer more braking surface. It's not necessary to switch from one braking side to the other brake side as frequently because, once sideways, they brake more efficiently. On a gigantic open slope, the longer skis are more comfortable.

It can be difficult to correctly judge the proper clothing. One might ski on a 45F or 55F degree day and roast in a fat cumbersome jacket. Or one might excitedly rush off to the slopes with light long johns under a shell only to encounter high winds and temperatures in the 20F's which will usually lead to getting sick.

I enjoy my one-piece suit and it can be difficult to estimate how much warmth it will or won't add to the clothing system. 20 years ago, in upstate New York, I ice climbed all day in 12F temperatures in my one-piece suit with no coat. I'd forgotten the jacket back home. I had a sore throat at the end of that day and went home the next day even though it was a Sunday.

Last Christmas I skied in upstate New York, same area, without warm enough leg coverings. I overestimated the warmth capability of my one-piece suit. On the 2d day I somehow managed to go out with even fewer leg layers on under the suit. I'd forgotten my heavy jacket in Virginia. I took my lunch break outside in the high wind. On the drive home my nose began to run. I thought, "Oh, the rental car has a smoke smell from a previous driver. That's why my nose has started running." Once home I went down with a sledgehammer of a flu that would have knocked me out of work except the worst day was on a Sunday.

Don't sit outside in the wind or rain during the lunch break. Last weekend I went inside and for the first time, took off the top of the one-piece suit, removed my jacket, and felt cool enough to enjoy sitting indoors for 1 hour. But beware of sitting at a waitress's booth for that long: she's trying to make a living. I gained 3 lbs. after eating a chili, cheeseburger, and fries (I didn't order the fries). Today I ordered a beer tube; sort of a sling that will hold beer cans. Perhaps with that I won't have to pay for $8 beers. If I stuff 3.8 oz. of bread in a pocket, I won't have to pay for lunch or dinner. Won't pay for it in out-of-control calories, either.

If one has a warm coat, insulated clothing under a warm, solid shell; a helmet, goggles covering their eyes, a neck gaiter, dry warm gloves, big plastic ski boots, if one's truly warm, then the wind on the ski lift ride doesn't feel uncomfortable. And if it starts snowing, it's a magical time. It's what sport's all about. It's snowing onto the shell, not melting, and the skis aren't harmed by it. It's romantic.

If a ski comes off, point the remaining ski sideways to not go backwards down or forwards down the hill, and clip the boot back into the ski binding. This must be on the uphill side. If one tries to clip into the ski on the downhill side, it will not work. Spin around and place the unclipped boot and ski on the uphill side.

I take 10 minutes breaks on the hour, from 50 minutes to the 60 minutes mark. Go to wherever there are seats. Sit there. If there's a gas fire pit with chairs around it, go there. Sit for 10 minutes. Eat a GU. Rest your boots on their heels. Stare at the people around you. Lower your heart rate. Hopefully you're dressed completely warmly and comfortably.

For my 1st 6-seasons I hadn't tried beer while skiing. One sees empty cans tossed from the lift towards trashcans sitting under the lift path. Or one used to see that, until the new owners removed the trashcans. I worried beer might cause a severe injury or beating from a ski or ski pole.

Update: last time out: 7-hour day, including a 1-hour lunch: sat in a booth, ordered a chili and cheeseburger and 3-beers. Fries arrived against my direct request.

They were delicious. Upon leaving lunch and returning to the lift line, I failed to properly turn sufficiently to view the upcoming chair at the lift station and the chair violently grabbed me and hurt my knee a little.

Then I saw a small mound of snow directly behind me; but thought the ski tails would cut through that mound but they didn't, and I took a moderately hard fall.

Then I slid at extremely slow speed into a downed snowboarder. No one was hurt. It was all slow motion. And later, in a backside lift line, I slid down a little slope and directly into a standing snowboarder. He was young and strong and saw me drifting his way. I gave up on my discipline of eating a GU every 30-minutes: I was stuffed from lunch. I gained 3 lbs. that day.

At some point, on a narrow long run, while skiing from side to side, I almost was hit by someone skiing down vertically from above to below. I heard them yell and felt them miss. This was before the lunch break.

But except for these mishaps, I fared well. The beer took the edge of my overall body pain from skiing 7-hours. And after that fall, I developed a laser focus about not turning with little mounds of snow behind me to catch the tail of my skis. That focus lasted hours, on each turn. I will never drink a beer except if

I have a designated driver to get me from the resort to back home.

A weekend later, I skied all day without beer and felt remarkably stronger and healthier at the end of the day than I had felt when beer fueled. Also, met a young strong skier on a chairlift who "started every day with a beer and ibuprofen." I'm sure he's making a mistake about the painkiller: don't take it.

By mid-season, I shifted gears: the downward slope appeared less steep, and I recovered previous seasons' ability to ski down in a 25-foot-wide column instead of skiing from one edge of the snow slope to the other edge of the snow slope. That was so enjoyable because then I didn't have to continually look upslope for faster (i.e., any other) skiers.

I listened to a distance runner on a podcast say, "the mountain flattened out for me;" she was referring to the steep slope become not so steep as she was running up it. I felt the same way; except for going down the slope: suddenly, it was less steep. This was on a blue. Suddenly it wasn't steep at all.

Always ski with a helmet. If nothing else, to avoid having another skier in a helmet collide with one's bare head. Also, if I'm down, to avoid catching a ski or snowboard to my bare head. And I bounced my helmeted head remarkably hard off the snow slope. Once I heard all the bones in my neck crack as I hit the ice with my helmet.

Unfortunately, I purchased an extra-large helmet. I'm not sure why I did that. I probably am a large or maybe even a medium. If I was to get a new helmet, I'd have to choose between a regular helmet: a helmet that plays music controlled by a cool-looking remote attached to the arm: or a triple rated helmet which would work for skiing, biking, and rock climbing. The music helmet would be best except sometimes one hears a scrape or woosh of a skier coming from above and that sound gives an important pre-collision warning.

Whatever helmet one purchases will be outdated after several years, so pick a neutral color. Avoid the bright yellow and red or shocking pink colors. They won't age as well.

After a big day on the slopes, visit a chiropractor. Some falls feel like sitting softly backwards into an easy chair. Other might be worse; for example, landing on the ribs with one arm extended above the head. That arm and elbow will feel weak the next day. It's not the arm. Yes, it feels as if it's the arm. But it's not; it's the neck. Get a treatment. I go weekly to a chiropractor or try to even when I'm not skiing.

On the last day of our season: (2 months ago, and out west they are still skiing and still getting snow); the local resort was down to 1 run. I might have avoided it had I known, but it turned out great. It was surely my biggest vertical day on the east coast. Naturally, I forgot to wear my altimeter watch.

As mentioned, there was simply the open 1 run, but it was the big run, from the top all the way to the bottom. It wasn't crowded. The snow park (jumps and rails) was gone. Being uncrowded meant there were no lines to get on the ski lift. I went on and on. And met a ski patrol expert on the lift; we were on the same lift twice.

The ski patrol expert said something about, "you can only ski so much," and explained how he enjoyed being a patrol member for socializing with the other members. In other words, skiing alone can't keep one happy: it has its limits. And I caught a glimpse of it for the 1st time on that day, probably in part because I was running down the same ski run all day. It gave me a glimpse of what might ultimately be waiting for one upon reaching the expert level.

Returning to backcountry skiing: the 2d outing on my Canadian adventure last month occurred after asking in Jasper about where to ski. A saleswoman told me many good areas were off limits due to people protesting about the rights of caribou- one assumes something to do with caribou migration routes. She told me to "Ski the Balds at Maligne Lake."

10-minutes later a stranger passed me. I asked him where a restaurant was, and he recommended one. Also, he recommended skiing the Balds at Maligne Lake. The next day I went there, fortunately seeing a ranger with a giant camera lens who told me, "Park in the lot on the left and ski the trail on the right." In the parking lot was a skier sitting in his car, waiting for his buddy. It was colder than I expected. Previously I had roasted and then frozen on the lake. So, on this 2d outing I left off the warm pants. But the cold forced me to reconsider. This required stripping off my 1-piece suit to put on the insulated pants and then redressing in the 1-piece suit. This was done in the back seat of the Jeep pickup truck. I was so eager to start the day but fiddled with my wardrobe quite a bit before starting up the trail.

The other 2 skiers gave me what advice they could, including that I should "Consider checking out the avalanche.ca website," which discusses current avalanche conditions. The skier said this with a concerned expression on his face that conveyed pity and fear for me. I informed him that I had been on the site. I hadn't of course, but I had perused the site back while sitting in my office, before the trip. I hadn't looked up the Balds at Maligne Lake the night before in the hotel, or ever.

But I knew that this winter was terrible for avalanches as early layers of snow had frozen hard and later, softer snow had fallen on top of the earlier frozen layers. Also, a salesman from Banff had chilled when I asked about ski touring the trail that one takes if one missed the left turn to try to summit Mt. Trundle. "No, no, avalanches are everywhere this year, and particularly on that trail. Go to avalanche.ca for more information."

Anyway, back to the parking lot, now dressed warmer, skis on, boots on, etc., I headed across the street and at a little hut I put on my skis. By now I'd figured out how to operate them heel free: happy days, "Look ma, I'm an expert." I went up the fire road, hour after hour. There were small black squirrels visible during my rest breaks. I found, after an hour or 2, that the fire road itself had been skied on enough so that there was a wide, hard, platform of snow. For example, I could sit on the road, and then stand back up on it by pushing against the road surface.

Off to the side of the road was unconsolidated snow: impossible to ski in or to regain one's stance once sat in. But the road had a reasonable and hard surface. At the side of the road was undisturbed powder.

I went along, hour after hour. My plan of a 1-hour lunch break was not feasible because it was too stinking cold. I'd be sweating with drops running down my ribs while skinning uphill, but cold by the end of the 10-minute break. Who knows what an hour of sitting would do to me. I began to take bigger breaks, all the while calculating that by the end of the day, I'd have taken a 1-hour lunch break, albeit dispersed into smaller segments: 25 minutes here instead of 10, or 20 minutes instead of 10, etc.

I mistakenly thought I was the only one skiing up the road that day, as evidenced by footsteps on top of ski tracks from long ago. I figured the 2 skiers had gone off somewhere on a milder circuit rather than risk the Balds. The tracks tricked me: it appeared that 2 people had hiked in boots on top of ski tracks from a week or 2 ago but the skiers had skied on top of the deep footprint tracks.

Finally, I came to a sign indicating a shortcut to the top or to the Balds. During this whole ascent I had been worried about the descent: would I be able to ski down or would it be too steep. Would I have to take off the skis and walk down, would I have to sidestep, would I have to keep my skins on, etc. Because I'm not a very good skier.

I had left a lunch-less hungry partner back in the hotel room. And I had taken a late start due to having to fill the jeep with gas, having remembered 30 minutes out that I forgot my gloves and returning to the hotel room to retrieve them, and because the Balds at Maligne Lake are 90 minutes (about 1 and a half hours) outside of town. No, there are no hotels closer to the Balds: only woods.

I took a few steps up the shortcut before realizing that descending the shortcut was going to be so challenging compared to operating on the fire road. The short cut was simply two ski tracks straight up or down the mountain: no room for turns. And I estimated that I'd run out of time before reaching the Balds. Unfortunately, I would not be able to risk my life skiing on an unstable avalanche slope for the sake of skiing in powder. I gave up on the shortcut and returned to the fire road.

I continued upwards on the fire road but finally chose the conservative decision to head back down. Despite misgivings, I removed the skins exposing the bare slippery waxed bottoms of my skis, thus allowing me to ski so much faster.

I was completely unsure of how I'd manage the descent. But it worked out wonderfully, if not chicken heartedly. Skiing the entire road "doing the pizza" to slow down was too tiring. I pointed one ski straight down the slope but into the powder off to side of the road and that powder slowed that ski down considerably. While the other ski was held in a sideways breaking position on the smoothed-out fire road.

By holding this pattern, I was able to slow my descent enough that I could ski down the entire road. Sometimes I shifted from one side of the road to the other, always aiming to stick 1 ski in the powder off the side of the road. Parts of the road near the end weren't so steep and I was able to point both skis straight down the road. And so, at least 1 ski at a time, I was skiing powder. At one point I took a break, and upon standing up, here came skiing straight down at rapid speed, in tracks in the powder, the 2 skiers I'd seen in the morning.

Alright, I had misread the footprints on the ski tracks in the morning. I wasn't the only one on the trail. I was completely sideways in my skis, blocking most but not all of the fire road. In front of my skis were 2 ski tracks in powder. I heard the 1st skier racing downhill. I thought he'd go behind me, but he stayed in the ski tracks inches in front of me. I was, as they say, pasmado (stunned, stupefied) and failed to back up. The 1st skier flew by right in front of my skis. The 2d skier yelled out, "a little help," meaning for me to back up a little bit. I didn't: again, stupefied.

From there, the slope was even less steep, and I made my way back to the parking lot in good time: the 2 skiers were waiting. I apologized for not moving out of their way and they were not at all agitated about that. I suspect they were waiting there to see if I would successfully descend the road or not. They were so friendly.

I asked about the width of their skis, and one had the same width as mine, "106mm at the waist, but probably different from yours at the tip and tail." Anything, I suppose, to distance his expert equipment from mine. The long drive back, my hotel key not working, the hungry partner by now well past lunch time not letting me into the room, getting the key updated at the hotel office, going out for Korean takeout, etc.

I had survived the day, I was alive. Unfortunately, I'd damaged both big toenails despite having tightened both boots down to their tightest settings. This meant that my boot set up was not acceptable. By the next day I sought help at the local shops mentioned earlier

I worried about my injured toenails because I wouldn't be able to continue to backcountry ski; not if it meant losing my toenails every time I tried it. But with help from 3 young experts, I think the equipment problems have been worked out. Unfortunately, skiing at the resort won't reveal flaws in my AT set up; it's necessary to get out and put in a long day in the mountains to check out the system.

There one has it: dress warmly, buy skis to avoid standing in line for 1 hour at the resort. I'd done that years ago with my kids. I didn't mind it then, but I would mind it now. Dress warm, have fun, learn at the resort. Yes, the 1st day out will be stressful, but doing it will train the body and before long you'll be passing me down the slopes.

Part 2

❖

KNEES

I skied for a few seasons and was nearing the end of a big season. I went outside to throw out the trash. I was wearing slides (slippers). I stumbled on some broken pavement, and it tweaked my knee. And then my knee began to hurt and then seriously hurt. And it would suddenly spark up at various times. It wasn't getting better.

This was right at the peak of the COVID scare. The gyms were closed. Forget about finding any workout equipment online: everything was sold out. I knew the knee flexion extension machine would help my knee.

To go way back; when I first started climbing at the New River, I remember 1 knee or the other aching during my long drives back from climbing there. And I found an ad in "The New Yorker" magazine that showed a knee flexion and extension weight bench. A former NFL football player featured in the ad explained how this bench exercise prevented "football knees."

So, I got the bench and used it. I was about 28 years old. And if I ever got a weight bench, I made sure it had the knee flexion/extension attachment. And I pretty much used that machine on and off, but mostly on, for decades. For much of the time I had a bench in my office. Back then it never occurred to me to put patients on it: it was for personal use only.

And it kept my knees from hurting. There were times when I got the bench out of my office to make for more space (I kept it in x-ray). And there were times when I shared an apartment or rented a room, and it was easier to use the leg machine at the gym than keep one in my residence. But I used it once or twice weekly.

Until the COVID scare, and the gyms were closed, and I skied too much, and stumbled, and injured my knee. I tried acupuncture. It helped: a little, it felt better: acupuncture is as powerful as it is indirect. But I'd step over a ladder laying on a porch and suddenly feel a lightning bolt pain jolt my knee. It was painful.

Eventually the online shortage lessened: I found a knee extension/flexion bench online before the gyms opened. Or perhaps the gyms opened first. And each time I used the machine, my knee improved. It still hurt, but it felt better. I went back to the regimen of doing knee extensions/flexions twice weekly. And, over the years, my knee improved so long as I do the flexion/extension exercise twice weekly, I feel perfect in my knees. Sometimes I'm too tired to do it, including last week (working with a cold). But almost always, if I feel well, I do it. I do acupuncture on my left knee twice weekly as well. I combine knee acupuncture with appetite reduction acupuncture, trying to reduce my weight. Years have rolled by and on most weeks, I hit the machine twice and do acupuncture twice weekly to help the knee.

On a ski lift recently, I sat next to a professor; perhaps at a college in Delaware; he was a biomedical knee neurosurgical professor or something. He did research and his big contribution to the world was to recommend exercise and weight loss to heal knees. Um, yes, if one can lose weight, it will help. I've been dieting for 20 years, and I've been heavier, and I've been lighter. I told him about the knee flexion/extension machine: he didn't seem impressed. I was nervous telling him lest the idea rocket across the nation and I be left without credit for it.

For knee extensions, start with a low weight, quite low, and slowly build up. I have kept it at 50 lbs. over the decades. It's not about strengthening the thigh muscles. If one puts the weight on 200 or 300 lbs., because that's what the thigh muscles can do, one can tear or damage the knee. So, keep it at 50 lbs. For the knee extensions. I worked up to 150 repetitions. Work up slowly if new to it; even if you're a weightlifter and especially if you're not.

For knee flexion (bending the knee backwards), keep it at ½ the reps and ½ the weight used for knee extension (straightening out the leg). So, 75 repetitions with 25 lbs. This must be worked up to, ever so slowly. Some weight machines at the gym might be so obviously easier or harder that the weight must be adjusted a little. For the flat bench in my office, I use 150 repetitions with 50 lbs. while seated. Then, I lay face down and reverse curl (flex) my knees 75 times with 25 lbs. of weight on the machine. No big deal, unless I forget to do it.

Sometimes I'll do these weights when I'm traveling, but often I won't. I returned from my 1st hand surgery in Thailand to a now retired MD's office here in northern Virginia. I hadn't done knee exercises or acupuncture to my knees during my trip; I was too busy with the operated-on hand. Finally, I went to the MD's office to remove the stitches from my hand. In anticipation of the suture removal, I had taken 2 painkillers from post-surgery medications.

Upon leaving my car and heading to the low red brick building of the MD, I noticed how remarkably more comfortable my knees felt from the pain killers.

And realized I had a soreness in my knees that I wasn't aware of because, anyway, they felt that way all the time. I hadn't done the knee flexion/extension during my time in Thailand and that explained the unusually uncomfortable soreness in my knees. The point being the knees might be sore and uncomfortable and one doesn't realize it since the pain's always present.

Sometimes after the knee extension/flexion, my knees feel a little bit sore in the afternoon. But by the day after, they feel distinctly better. For the first year or 2 after the injury, while skiing, I could always feel that left knee getting a little sore. And I still view the right knee as stronger than the left knee. But for now, neither knee hurts. So, stick with the knee flexion and extension twice weekly. Add acupuncture twice weekly or at least regularly.

Usually, once weekly I hit the gym for a leg day: which occurs every 4th day at the gym. It's a day for legs only; one rests the arms. I do some squats, a leg press, and then the leg extension and flexion machines. Since I'm at the gym, I'll do some crunches. That's been my leg day workout for decades.

Part 3

Use orthotics: get SPS/Foot Levelers from a chiropractor. They make these in ¾ length or full length. These tactically and statically support the arches in the foot. That big arch in the foot will flatten out over time; because of the weight bearing down from the body onto the foot; and from the foot standing on flat hard surfaces: "poured concrete." If we walked on a beach or on turf, orthotics would be less necessary. Perhaps we wouldn't need them at all.

The shin bone goes into the ankle joint at a right angle, at a 90-degree angle. The one's perpendicular to the other. Such a meeting of bones occurs very rarely in the body. It allows for the body weight to crush out the foot arches. People who weigh 130 lbs. or less can go without orthotics. Maybe 140 lbs., or 150 lbs.; I'm not sure of the exact cut off. The rest of us need them. I must have them for my knees. Once the foot flattens out, the angle of the shin bone changes to follow the collapse of the arch. This shift in the shin bone transfers to an unequal stress where the shin bone meets the thigh bone.

The shin bone presents a table, the tibial plateau, which the thigh bone rests upon. If the plateau tilts to one side, there will be knee trouble. Stand barefoot on a hard surface; let the foot arch sink low; now arch it up high: note how the shin bone rotates to follow the height of the arch. This change in position of the shin bone ends up affecting the top of the shin bone where it forms the tibial plateau – the tabletop comprising the lower half of the knee joint. If the tibial plateau isn't level, there will be knee pain.

The knee joint is a ginglymus joint; meaning, it's a hinge joint: think of door hinge. It's not built for excessive leeway. It's not a loose joint such as the shoulder or wrist. It goes straight forward and straight backwards. Standing around on it with the lower half tilted to one side will hurt. Fix this by wearing orthotics.

Foot Levelers tout themselves as being the best orthotics because they have 3 bumps to support the 3 arches of the foot. There are other hard orthotics which basically consists of a heel cup and a flowing hard arch which supports the big foot arch. These are better than nothing, better than no orthotic at all. But there's the little arch on side of the foot, and a slightly larger arch under the ball of the foot that the hard arches essentially ignore.

Sometimes these hard arch supports are extremely expensive. It's a rare case of something costing more but not being as good.

The Foot Levelers orthotics can have a heel wedge to combat foot pronation or supination. The company will put this in depending upon the mold of the foot. They can also build a little horseshoe ring of support around the outside of the heel to relieve heel spurs.

A full length orthotic will give more cushioning and support than a ¾ length orthotics but be careful that the toes have room in the front of the shoe if they are sitting on top of an orthotic. Mostly I used ¾ length orthotics in my dress shoes but a full length orthotic in my tennis shoes. I have a pair of tennis shoes I wear when lifting weights in the gym: those have full length orthotics. For ski boots or ice climbing boots, I usually stick in ¾ length orthotics. And I remove the orthotics once winter's over.

For decades I took a pair of Teva sandals to the cobbler, and he glued a pair of ¾ length orthotics onto them: put the back heel of the orthotic exactly lined up to the back heel of the Tevas. I hiked all day in them. I wore them mountaineering in the Tetons, Canadian

Rockies, and while climbing in Joshua Tree, California and West Virginia. But my feet swelled during weekends carrying the heavy pack while rock climbing in West Virginia. Somehow a shoe (with orthotics inside) gives feet more support than the Tevas alone. But I could still wear the Tevas as a casual shoe. And they are a deal at $40. Some Tevas are more expensive, but they curl upwards on the edges causing gravel and grit to collect in them and not fall out.

In later years, I've moved from Teva sandals to water shoes. The Teva company makes them, as does Keene, or many other companies. It's an open aired sandal that includes a toe cap. Maybe my 64-year-old size 15 feet look a little better covered up somewhat. I can hike for hours in these shoes. I usually end up wearing socks with these to keep the orthotic from rubbing up against the bottom of my foot.

The orthotics stay glued onto the sandal or water shoe for the life of the shoe. I don't wear them in water as water would loosen the orthotic glue job. I try not to spend too much time in the rain in these sandals or water shoes. Sometimes they get rained on a little.

If one gets an orthotic into a tennis shoe, one achieves the ultimate weight bearing situation. Also, it's important to have orthotics in a shoe while biking, especially if the bike shoe clips into the bike pedal. If on vacation, avoid pedaling a boat or bike barefoot, lest you suffer a stress fracture on the foot.

Don't wear a big, hard plastic ski boot (or ice climbing boot) without a custom orthotic.

Part 4

Keep shoe heel level and new. For expensive dress shoes, ask a cobbler to place heel taps on the outside heel of the shoe. This will prevent the heel from wearing down unevenly. Once that occurs, it's as if someone stuck a little wedge under the foot and this will transfer unequal force to the knee joint.

Some big, rangy, tough legged people can wear boots that are worn down without hurting their knees. I don't know how this happens. Ignore them. Keep your heels level.

I prefer steel heel taps to nylon heel taps. Sometimes the steel heel taps slip on a hard surface, especially a hard wet surface, for example, on the hard floor of a shopping mall, a store in a mall, or on the hard floor of the gym near the exit. Nylon heel taps won't slip but they must be replaced quite regularly.

If I'm walking on a sidewalk with nylon heel taps, I feel them grinding away with every step. I used nylon heel taps for years on my dress shoes before the cobbler finally replaced them with new steel heel taps.

I had steel taps put onto the heels of my Timberland hiking boots. One eventually tore off and the cobbler replaced it. Get them onto the boot heel while it's new.

Sometimes while walking in a library or hallway a woman will ask me if I'm wear dancing taps on my shoes. The steel taps can make a distinctive clicking noise while walking. I pretend they are spurs and I'm a cowboy.

Don't walk on someone's nice, polished hardwood floor while wearing steel heel taps. Take off your shoes even if the gracious host assures you that it's not necessary. They are underestimating the scratching the steel taps will put onto the floor.

The steel heel taps will wear a hole in cheap floor mats in your car. Find some old Lexus mats from a junked Lexus and stick those on your driver's side car floor.

I slip a little while wearing steel heel taps but have learned to walk gingerly on hard tile surfaces. If ever I fall from slipping on them, I might reconsider using them; but for now, I prefer them to replacing the nylon taps.

A well-made dress shoe will have a solid oak or rubber heel. These shoes can offer healthy support for decades. The heel will stay level if protected with a heel tap. Probably a dress shoe that costs $300 or more, which sounds expensive; but as they look great and can last through 10 or 20 years of hard use, they are a bargain.

Tennis shoes have that soft cushy heel that makes them ideal for running. Over time, the heel will pack down, leaving an uneven heel pad under the foot. Do not go by the tread on the bottom of the tennis shoe, as the heel will pack down on the side long before the tread shows signs of wear.

In the womb, the leg starts out facing backwards. It slowly turns around to face forward. But never quite makes it all the way; it's normal for the foot to point a little to the outside. In the average person's gait, the heel strike occurs slightly on the outside of the heel. And in a tennis shoe, that zone will pack out. There's no point putting a heel tap on a tennis shoe as the soft cushy heel material will pack out regardless.

Once this happens, the shoe will hurt the knee, back, or foot. Wear tennis shoes for 60 days (about 2 months) before replacing them. I refer to 60 days of wearing them; track it in an excel worksheet or in a notebook. This means I don't want expensive tennis shoes. Also, I'm 203 lbs.; a lighter person may get more days from their tennis shoes. Unfortunately, this also applies to hiking boots that have a soft, hollow, non-replaceable heel. Those boots are great when new but will eventually pack out the side of the heel, same as a tennis shoe. So, avoid spending $270 on a hiking boot that cannot be reheeled.

The Timberland boots have solid heels, and this allows them to sport a heel tap. Danner boots, at least some models, have a solid heel that allows the placement of a heel tap on them. The new style boots that are a cross between a tennis shoe and hiking look great but won't be anatomically supportive after 600 miles or 60 days of use. Don't break the bank on such a shoe: it's better to spend less and replace the shoe with a new pair once it breaks down.

Any shoe will require nice tight laces to support the foot. Don't run in loose shoes. Don't walk in them. If one's slipping into and out of their tennis shoes, get ready for knee pain. It's best to snugly lace up the shoe each time upon wearing it.

None of this applies to lightweight slippers or flip flops: wear them until the soles are gone. There's no heel to remain under one side of the foot once the other side of the heel has worn away. I've been wearing the same slipper/slide house sandal for 7 years and won't replace them. The foot doesn't get compressed into a flip flop. It's almost the same as going barefoot except the sole of foot doesn't have to contact the floor.

Back in the 1970's we were all enthusiastic about walking around barefoot. I took off for a hike on a paved road with a buddy. I went barefoot, thinking anyway, if my feet get sore, it will toughen them up. That was an error. Be careful of walking around barefoot outside. I picked up some lumps and a wart on the sole of my feet from doing that. I'm probably never going to have those bumps surgically removed. It would be nice to have normal, smooth, unflawed soles.

To summarize, to heal your knees: (1) do the seated flexion and extension weights, (2) wear orthotics, (3) keep shoes relatively new or equipped with heel taps, (4) get regular acupuncture, (5) take a joint support nutrition such as chondroitin sulfate, and (5) always wear your shoes snugly laced.

I never bothered replacing or protecting the heels on my bike shoes as they clip into the bike pedals using a metal cleat. I don't walk around much in them. I haven't swapped the heel on my ski boots out for the same reason: they clip into a ski binding. I walk in them only from the parking lot to the ski slope. Some boots have a replaceable heel strike area; it might be a good idea to replace it, but ski boots are so uncomfortable to walk in that I don't worry much about the heel strike zone.

Eventually ice climbing boots might need to be re-heeled if one hikes many miles in them. I usually toss sandals and water shoes about as frequently as tennis shoes, although their heels might be thicker and made of a more solid rubber.

EPILOGUE

In final summary, to be clear; Canadians would scoff at my getting lost on their lake: my errors were so numerous as to be laughable to a competent skier. However, please, if you are new to mountains, don't charge along as I did in the above narrative. Many of my close calls were survivable due to a lifetime spent backpacking and climbing, miserably failing and struggling in mountains, big and small, since I was a teenager. Take it slow; don't charge in over your head; keep your personal safety paramount in all adventures. The mountains are going to be full of extremely close calls even if you take it incrementally slowly, barely going into any risky situation. The mountains have teeth. Don't assume, because I was inept in my journeys, that a beginner can or should leap onto glaciers or snowy mountains.

www.ingramcontent.com/pod-product-compliance
Lightning Source LLC
LaVergne TN
LVHW051955060526
838201LV00059B/3664